The Hat Box

PUTTING on the MIND of CHRIST

PATSY CLAIRMONT

W PUBLISHING GROUP™

www.wpublishinggroup.com

A Division of Thomas Nelson, Inc.
www.ThomasNelson.com

The Hat Box
© 2003 by Patsy Clairmont

Published by W Publishing Group, a Division of
Thomas Nelson, Inc., Nashville, Tennessee 37214.

Scripture quotations in this book are from *The New King
James Version* © 1984 by Thomas Nelson, Inc.
unless specified otherwise.

Other Scripture quotations are from *The Holy Bible,
New International Version* (NIV) © 1973, 1984 by
International Bible Society, used by permission of
Zondervan Publishing House.

ISBN 0-8499-1797-2

Printed in the United States of America
03 04 05 06 PHX 5 4 3 2

My hats off to you, darling Justin.
Thank you for making me a Nana.

Contents

Hats Off to . . .

Okay, let me get this out of the way right up front—I own twelve hats. I know because I just counted. Don't get me wrong; I love hats. I just don't own many because I don't wear them.

Well, that's not exactly true. I try to wear them, but I'm built real close to the sidewalk, like a gnome, and putting a roof on a short structure can create a comical effect. I know this from the guffaws I've generated when I've stepped out in public with my head tucked up inside my baseball cap. It's not the ball cap that tickles people because I get the same reaction when I'm arrayed in my straw hats, my winter caps, or my garden head-gear. The snickers would offend me, but I caught a glimpse of myself in a store's window as I sashayed by, and I could be a ringer for Granny from *The Beverly Hillbillies.* Personally, I thought she was cute.

I've imagined myself swishing across the room like Audrey Hepburn in *Breakfast at Tiffany's* (ask your mother), flapping my eyelashes under the wide brim of a picture hat. Alas, I'm grateful to stumble—hatless—across the room in time for breakfast.

I have friends who wear hats majestically. My hat's off to them. They have considerable stature (doesn't bother me, doesn't bother me, doesn't bother me), long necks (mine is full of chins), and eyes the size of portholes.

While this book is about hats, it's about so much more. We'll check out what's going on inside our hats . . . our thought life. What sort of thinking deserves a hats-off salute from us? And what kind of thinking do we want to keep under our hats?

The first book in this series, *The Shoe Box,* dealt with how we walk. *The Hat Box* considers the way we think, which takes us from the tip of our painted toes to the top of our (oops, pointed) heads.

We will don twelve "consider" verses from Scripture—just as we would put on our favorite hats—that we might experience the Lord's voice in surround-sound, filling our minds with divine counsel. Each verse will have a corresponding head covering to help us to remember to "think up." The Lord tells us to "set your mind on things above" (Colossians 3:2), and that's just what we're going to do.

So pull out your hat boxes. If they're like mine, you'll need to dust them off, and let's consider how our minds influence everything we do.

Okay, girlfriends, grab your tams, fezzes, berets, sombreros, hoods, caps, babushkas, derbies, stocking caps, and beanies, and let's head out . . .

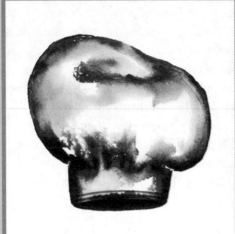

Our world needs some folks willing
to cause a stir with love!

❧ Chef's Hat ❧

CONSIDER ONE ANOTHER

*Consider one another in order to stir up love and
good works. (Hebrews 10:24)*

What's cooking?

My friend Ann is a personal chef, and
she is in my kitchen stirring up love while I write.
In fact, I consumed some of her loving efforts for
lunch—a scrumptious, stuffed pepper. Because I'm
moving at breakneck speed until Thanksgiving, my
husband and I splurged and asked Ann to whip
up some dinners for our freezer. That way, even
when I'm traveling, Les has easy access to a meal,
and when I'm home, especially on the nights I'm
working on a book deadline, we just toss one of
her tasty offerings in the oven. Ann ran a retail
business for years called Somewhere in Time but

had a longing to touch people's lives in a more personal way. Now under the name Dinner on Time, she is cooking for handicapped folks, working mothers, widows, widowers, and individuals who are pressed on all sides with responsibilities that pull them out of the kitchen. Her efforts bless others. I can attest to that.

My friend Ginny and her married daughter Erin both wear chefs' hats several times a month when they host "Two Hearts of Gold." They team-cook in Ginny's home, teaching young mothers simple yet sumptuous meals for their families. The pair gives tips and fixes the food as their guests gather round to watch. Then the participants have the joy of eating what Ginny and Erin have prepared. How fun is that? They also teach how to set a lovely table with the finishing touches of flowers from the garden and candles from the cupboard. Truly these two ladies are stirring up love.

I'm not surprised because Ginny has been a cherished friend for years, and many times she has baked my favorite concoction—mashed potato rolls—and delivered them to me. More than once she has put the dough in her car to rise as she drove two hours to visit my home. One time the temperatures were scorching, and by the time she arrived, the dough had risen right out of its container, crawled over the headrest, oozed under the seatbelt, and was resting comfortably in the seat. It looked like the blob that ate Philly. But once it was contained and baked, it melted in one's mouth like soft butter.

I would be hard-pressed to tout a chef's hat without those who know me giggling themselves silly. While I enjoy cooking in spurts (but then, who eats spurts?), it's not one of my gifts. For one thing, I'm far too exacting for it to be fun. I'm more like a rocket scientist—minus the brains.

I do love recipes, though. You would think, judging by my stack of cookbooks, that I must be a gourmet cook. Or maybe I think the books give the illusion of cookness. My favorite cookbooks are by Susan Branch. I love the way she incorporates her art throughout the instructions. It stirs up the artisan within me, which I hope will then pour over into the batter as I clatter about the kitchen.

How do you stir up love?

Barbara Johnson, beloved speaker, writer, and friend to many (including me), was diagnosed with a brain tumor more than a year ago. Many individuals sent Barb cards, letters, and gifts. Countless numbers of people prayed for her, wired flowers, and paid visits. Folks were generous, and Barbara was touched.

One group of people found a unique way to stir up love for her. They realized Barb's surgery meant she had to have her head shaved, so they threw her a hat shower. She received a plethora of headgear—big hats, fancy ones, fun ones, and colorful headscarves.

I loved that idea not only because the hats would be useful but also because Barb has a history with hats. She is the author of many books, including the classic, *Stick a Geranium in Your Hat and Be Happy.*

Obviously many people think of hats when they think of Barbara. She told me that some years ago she was invited to speak in a large church, and because of her hat reputation, most of the women attending came wearing head coverings. And some were pretty outrageous. Women wore hats with tall feathers, fluffy birds, twiggy nests, and faux jewels. One lady even wore a bedpan filled with a miniature garden sprouting atop her noggin. Barb said the pastor came out to introduce her but was startled to see a sea of extravagant headgear filling his sanctuary. He looked all around and said, "I can't do this. Barb, introduce yourself." He then walked off the stage chuckling and wagging his head in disbelief while the ladies erupted into life-giving gales of laughter. (Guys just don't get it.)

No wonder the women teamed up to give Barb a hat shower in her time of need; she had been stirring up love in others' lives for years.

As Barb knows, loving people is more than an emotion. If our minds don't support our emotions in caring for others, our feelings of love will thin out into just good intentions. Often loving others is inconvenient. We need the strength of our mind to help to solidify our commitment to other people. Otherwise we will become one of the multitudes reciting, "I meant to do something, but I just never got around to it." I've uttered that excuse more times than I'd like to count. How about you?

Sarah Trollinger is a woman who isn't offering excuses but is extending help. A former schoolteacher, Sarah made a decision seventeen years ago to help troubled teens, and she has stayed true to that task. No regrets for her. Today Sarah heads up House of Hope, a Christian residential program for troubled boys and girls ages fourteen to seventeen in Orlando, Florida. Thousands of teens have had their lives turned around at this ten-acre facility.

I've met a number of the young people from House of Hope and have heard their stirring testimonies. These kids have known the worst of life, but with the support of Sarah and her staff, they are experiencing new beginnings.

Because of the Christ-centered approach and the devoted workers, House of Hope has an unheard-of 95 percent success rate in seeing the teens change directions. Way to stir up love and good works, Sarah. My chef's hat is off to you!

Each of us might do it differently, but we're all called to invest in others. It's a decision worth making, whether you're mixing up a batch of cookies, supporting friends through hardships, touching the life of a young person, or _____(you fill in the blank).

Let's rally, girlfriends. Our world needs some folks willing to cause a stir with love!

I'm not sure if the striking contrast between the yellow hard hat and my mushy green face inspired my tour guide, but he thought we shouldn't stay long.

~ Hard Hat ~

CONSIDER OUR SOURCE
OF STRENGTH

*Consider now, for the LORD has chosen you to build . . . be
strong, and do it. (1 Chronicles 28:10)*

A number of years ago I spoke at a church that was building a new facility. I was asked if I would like to tour the construction site, so out of curiosity and good manners I agreed. When we arrived, my eyes were the size of dinner plates. I had never seen such a church. I was a small-town girl used to little white buildings sporting spires in Currier and Ives settings. This megastructure was the size of Rhode Island. Or so it seemed to me. I was handed a hard hat and cautioned to step carefully. The head covering was to protect me from falling debris.

I was informed that only the church board had seen the site, so I felt special and rather official to be chosen for this viewing. That is, until they took me up a temporary elevator and then onto scaffolding to look down several stories into the Grand Canyon-sized sanctuary. My quivering lips wanted to yell out, "I don't do heights!" But I didn't want to seem unappreciative of the honor bestowed on me. Besides, by now anxiety had squeezed all the air out of my lungs, and I couldn't have whispered much less screamed. I just kept telling myself that with Jesus I could do this.

I'm not sure if the striking contrast between the yellow hard hat and my mushy green face inspired my tour guide, but he thought we shouldn't stay long. Later I wished they had given me the hard hat. I would have bronzed it as a trophy to remind me of the time I wobbled onto skyscraper planks and leaned over to see the foundations far below, all the time feeling like I would drown in my fear. But I lived to tell about it.

That's the thing about most of my personal victories: They're characterized by knee-knocking fear amidst God's empowering strength. What an oxymoron. God asks us to build—whether character within us or a supportive structure for others. I used to think that meant when I was afraid, if I prayed for God to quiet my nervous nature, I would be able to step out calmly in His power. And I have experienced times in which I was physically, emotionally, and spiritually in alignment. But more often than not I've prayed, and my knees have continued to ricochet off each other like cymbals. I've stumbled forward only to find on the other side of my adversity that I had made it in spite of my noisy insecurities and because of Jesus' faithful presence.

That bit of insight changed the information stored under my hard hat. I realized I couldn't allow my fluttering heart to determine what I would or would not do. So what if my hands trembled, my eye twitched, or my palms moistened? Most victories come with a price tag attached. Besides, momentary physical and emotional quivering seem like a small price to pay for building internal strength. Of course, I find that easier to write than to remember when I'm in the midst of a challenge.

Some of you will understand when I confess that I find entertaining in my home a challenge. I'm a hyper-homemaker prior to my guests' arrival. I love when people visit, but for days before that I stampede through the house like a crazed stallion, nostrils flaring, mane whipping in the wind, whinny-ing directions to anyone who will listen, while great beads of sweat collect on my coat. I can't seem to get it through my hard head much less my hard hat to relax and enjoy the process.

And have you noticed that most of life is a process of building a firm foundation within ourselves? A friend called today to give me an update on her life. Her family has been through untold hardships for almost two years with almost no letup. They have become veteran hard hat wearers. As I listened to her combat report, I thought about my frenzy over houseguests. That was a reality check for me.

I decided to create a blueprint that would help my friends and me know how to build strong struc-ture within ourselves. We can tuck this plan under our hard hats to pull out in time of need.

Uptight? Lower personal expectations. High stan-dards are admirable, but perfectionism is depleting and defeating. Our worth isn't in our performance. Our worth isn't in our performance. Our worth isn't in our performance. Frenzy eats energy and devours joy. Try meditating on verses about grace . . . then extend some to yourself.

Overcommitted? Sometimes maturity means

confessing your mistake of taking on too much and backing out of the overload. Yes, some folks won't be happy; that's their decision. And remember, delegating is a sign of wisdom not weakness.

Jumpy? Are you getting enough rest? Sleep helps to restore balance, renew outlook, and improve concentration. Meds are available that can help to break the cycle of exhaustion until you can get back into healthy sleep patterns.

Feeling lost? Seek counsel. Extended problems bring a lingering stress load. Visiting with a counselor can help you to see how you're internalizing your situation and give you a clearer perspective. Support groups and prayer groups are also helpful survival tools.

Life out of whack? Balance activities. If you're sitting a lot, take brisk, fifteen-minute walks. If you're highly active, take twenty-minute bubble baths.

Overtaxed? Prioritize your strength. Do what must be done first, and when necessary, let other things go. They'll wait for you. Trust me.

These tips won't solve your dilemmas, but they will help you to survive them.

Wherever we are in our lives, we need to consider that God asks us to build. I have to remind myself that it's not my job to tear down, criticize, or murmur but to build. And while I often feel fragile, I'm instructed to be strong and build. That's where my weakness in His strength equals lasting results.

So join me, friends, in putting on our hard hats. Life can be like walking a narrow plank in a high place, and while that might be out of our comfort zone, think of the views!

Our Enduring Captain's compass is aligned perfectly, and He directs even the eagle's path.

Captain's Hat

CONSIDER RESILIENCY

*Consider Him who endured . . . lest you become weary
and discouraged in your souls. (Hebrews 12:3)*

Recently Les and I went on a cruise to Alaska as part of my speaking calendar. How fun is that?! For one week we were a virtual floating conference.

With anticipation, Les and I planned and packed. In fact, at one point I had two friends join me in the packing process to make sure I thought of everything.

If you've taken a cruise, you know that several dinners are designated as "formal wear" and several as "dress wear." By the time you've packed your absolutely dressy, sort of dressy, and not at all dressy clothes, your suitcases bulge. Then, of course, you need pool wear, what-if-it-gets-cold wear, and don't forget underwear. And that's not all. I had to have speaking outfits, a fishing outfit, and backup outfits for all of the above. Top that off with my shoe wardrobe and a small cache of hats—including a captain's hat in case he needed advice. Oh, yes, add the library of books I was going to catch up on, as well as my computer. Then Les had the audacity to want space in one of our three suitcases for his stuff. Men. What was he thinking?

Our excursion took place one month before Les and I celebrated our fortieth wedding anniversary, so we designated the cruise as our gift to each other. It was a trip we had dreamed of for years.

All aboard! (Wait, I think that's the call for trains.)

Ship ahoy! (Hmm, are those cookies?)

Anyway, off we went, cutting through the deep blue seas.

Les and I do well with motion, yet strangely, after we set sail, neither of us felt quite right. Les spent most of the following day in our room ill. The day after that I joined him. Bottom line: We spent the cruise in our cabin with a mean virus. Not a fun travel companion. It gave us lots of time, though, to stare at all my unnecessary packing.

Toward the end of the cruise, Les disembarked

at a port for a half-hour and returned with a faux fur jacket and matching headgear for me. I was shivering from chills and immediately wrapped up in the coat and pulled on the fuzzy hat. I looked like an ailing coyote, but the warmth of the gear was comforting and Les's thoughtfulness endearing. Together we wobbled out onto the deck and listened to the icebergs moan. (Or was that me?)

Just as I deliberately pulled on that hat, Les and I found we had to purpose to pull on grateful thoughts to protect our minds during the cruise so we didn't allow our discouragement to dictate the overall quality of our trip. We decided early on in our sickness to think of the ship as our personal hospital, and we had to admit we had never been in one with better views. We also decided that having ready-made meals available around the clock was better than one of us having to drag out of our feverish bed to smear grape jam on a slab of stale bread.

One morning while 90 percent of the passengers had gone ashore to participate in an excursion to photograph wildlife up close and personal, I dragged my aching body up to the ship's salon for a pedicure. As I sat there, I could feel myself dropping into a pool of self-pity, and I realized I needed to once again shore up my mind. So, between coughs and sniffles, I thanked the Lord for the sweet girl who was tending to my tootsies and for the lovely water view out the plate-glass windows in front of me.

That's when an eagle soared by not twenty feet from me. I almost jumped out the window with excitement. I had never seen an eagle before, which was obvious to the salon workers, who giggled at my antics. I couldn't say much because I had laryngitis, but my arms were flailing in all directions.

And guess what?

Not ten minutes later another eagle swept by. No kidding. The cruise folks told me the feathered fellows don't usually fly so close to the ship while at port. I think God knew that I would need His loving intervention in duplicate. With the second sighting a verse flew into my thoughts: "But those who wait on the LORD shall renew their strength; they shall mount up with wings like eagles, they shall run and not be weary, they shall walk and not faint" (Isaiah 40:31).

Virus or no virus, I felt uplifted. I realized I didn't have to leave the ship to be appreciative of God's care for me or to have a great time. God honors even the tiniest of efforts to think His way. And He is compassionate toward us when we're weary and discouraged.

Do you need an eagle sighting today? Ask God for one. It may come in the form of an unexpected visitor, a cheerful phone visit, an inspiring song, the right book, a comforting dream, or verses that wing into your mind and nest.

Of course, we all know some times are discouraging, and no eagles are in sight. In truth, some seasons we scan the skies, and the only things in flight are ominous clouds thundering intimidating threats, and we, wearied, have to hunker down and ride out the storm. But eventually every storm subsides, every sky clears, and all winds still.

The important truth to consider is who navigates our ship regardless of the swirling circumstances. Our Enduring Captain's compass is aligned perfectly, and He directs even the eagle's path. He reads the skies, rides the waves, and guides us into safe harbors. And guess what? He doesn't need our advice. Now there's a captain worth trusting.

All aboard!

*Let's plop on our party hats,
put our heads together and consider
what great things God does.*

~ Party Hat ~

CONSIDER FRIENDSHIPS

Consider what great things He has done for you.
(1 Samuel 12:24)

Some folks are worth throwing a shindig for . . . like my childhood chum, Carol. She and I love celebrating just about everything. But with the flurry of life, we find just having time together is reason enough to break out the party hats.

Many summers ago Carol and I were into hats big time. Or should I say, big-time hats. I still giggle when I see our teenage pictures. Carol's hat looked like exotic palm fronds atop stilts (she's tall) while mine appeared to be a gargantuan lampshade with feet (I'm . . . uh . . . not so tall). At the time we thought we were cool.

Then we went through the black headscarf era. We looked like a couple of mournful waifs. I'm grateful to say the hooded fashion fad was short-lived.

As young mothers, our sons were born four months apart, and Carol and I regularly topped off their outfits with hats. Those sons are now nearing forty (eek!), and they are both hat wearers. "Train up a child . . ."

Not long ago Carol and I again bought hats together. Far more conservative headgear this time, rather tea-party looking; yet I could tell by the way we were strutting past the mirror, we still thought we were cool. And one of the coolest things about us, we believe, is our friendship.

Forty-six years (golly) have passed since Carol and I met in junior high school. ("Hi, my name is Patsy. Wanna be friends?" I mean, how could she resist?) We have throughout the years giggled and cried, grieved and celebrated, schemed and dreamed. We have vacationed together, cared for and about each other's children, guarded each other's secrets, prayed for each other's welfare, and heralded the joy of grandmother-hood. We've studied Scripture together, helped gussy up each other's homes, and shared in feasts at each other's tables.

We're aware that God has done great things in our lives and one of those things is our enduring friendship. Friendships with history become more valuable through time. Trust and security build when you understand the other person is committed to the relationship even through blustery seasons. Carol and I have survived misunderstandings, hurt feelings, crises, and separation.

We have withstood relational pressures not because our hearts are naturally expansive but because Jesus has been growing us up. And don't you think that's one of the purposes of relationships? Stop and think about it. Who are the most cherished people in your life? What have you survived together? Haven't those experiences honed your understanding of each other's hearts and devotion, and hasn't enduring difficulties shone shafts of light on your own heart, exposing its contents? Yes, while personal interactions with others can be painfully revealing, they also can be enriching.

Ralph Waldo Emerson said, "The glory of friendship is not the outstretched hand, nor the kindly smile, nor the joy of companionship; it's the spiritual inspiration that comes to one when he discovers that someone else believes in him and is willing to trust him with his friendship."

Let's plop on our party hats, put our heads together, and consider what great things God does through people who risk being involved with others. And risk is exactly what relationships require. Anyone who has experienced a jealous relative, an unfaithful spouse, a critical boss, a cantankerous neighbor, a belligerent salesclerk, a haughty teenager, or a gossipy friend knows that.

Regardless of your age you've probably run into people issues. Mine began in infancy when I bellowed for attention and folks didn't immediately sprint to my cradle. Know what I mean? Left to our humanity, we tend to be self-serving in how we relate and what we expect from others.

I'm thankful that Jesus set a new standard for relationships when He showed Himself to be a servant and a friend. Servanthood and friendship are excellent handholding, girlfriend attributes. It's hard to separate the two when one is longing for and working toward healthy relationships, whether that be mother-child, husband-wife, or employee-boss.

I realize when I'm willing to internally acquiesce to another—only if it's appropriate and loving—that response benefits us both. That might mean giving up my right to be right. Ouch! Now that smarts. Yet mentally, relationally, and spiritually, that's a smart response. Or it could mean I need to pull back in the shadows, allowing another to take bows in the limelight. Then again, it might mean allowing another to lead even when I know I could do it better.

Golly, this relational stuff is heady. "Heady" in that I need to think through if being right is my top priority. If so, then I'm going to be like a bird on an ice floe—lonely and in need of fuzzy slippers. If I expect to be the center of all conversations, I'll be disappointed and avoided. And if I'm a demanding control freak, my circle of influence will narrow, and my internal life will tighten into a tummy-tucking knot.

I'm so grateful Jesus enables me to change, one groaning effort at a time, and I'm thankful for those folks in my life who have given me the space and time to change. It's easy (but not loving) to view a person in one light and then mentally to lock them into never being different. When that happens, even if the individual changes, she might feel bound to her old behavior when in our predetermined presence. Grace is a liberating quality—no, let me restate that. Grace is a required quality for family members, mates, moms, servants, and friends. Grace is a wide space, acreage full of forgiveness, humility, acceptance, safety, and love.

When I consider what great things the Lord has done for me, grace and friendships make me want to break out bags of confetti, kazoos, and my most outrageous party hat. Let the party begin!

*My most requested medication
as a kid was pudding.*

Nurse's Cap

CONSIDER GOD'S COMPASSION

Consider my affliction and deliver me. (Psalm 119:153)

My mom was my favorite nurse. Oh, she wasn't a professional nurse, but she sure was a compassionate one. She seemed to excel at nurseness. We moms usually are nurses by default. We fluff pillows, clean body parts, dispense medications, remove splinters, and soothe feverish brows.

I learned the gentle touch of caregiving by observing Mom, who knew how to bolster an ailing child's spirit. My most requested medication as a kid was pudding, which she administered generously. But mostly when I was ill I just wanted to be well. I thought Mom should deliver me from my afflictions—now. She sure tried her best.

However, once Mom attempted to turn in her nurse's badge. (Do nurses have badges?) My sister-in-law, while visiting my parents, went into labor with her third child. Things progressed more rapidly than she anticipated, and by the time my sister-in-law made it to the car for the trip to the hospital, she realized the baby was about to make her appearance. My brother shuffled his wife back into the house and called an ambulance, but before it arrived, little Susan was born with Mother, wide-eyed, standing there. Mom, who usually was undaunted by life, obviously was rattled. After that nerve-racking blessing, she lost a lot of her desire to don her nurse's cap but instead shuttled any of us who were ailing to the nearest doctor.

Nursing isn't an easy profession, which is probably why it wasn't on my list of what I wanted to be when I grew up. My lineup included wishes like ballerina and Calamity Jane—both of which, had I pursued them, would have meant I needed—you guessed it—a nurse. Spinning, as in pirouette, definitely makes me dizzy (okay dizzier) and just thinking about saddling ol' Smokey makes me ah-ah-choo!

So even though I didn't want to be a nurse, I

appreciate them. I find most of them pursued their career in medicine out of a desire to help the hurting, even if their patients come in small, furry bundles.

My friend Janet, out of a grateful heart, invited a couple of nurses for lunch. They were women who had befriended her and her husband, Loch, during his recent long hospitalization. To be treated tenderly and professionally when one is desperately ill and vulnerable is a blessing you don't soon forget. Loch won't.

While enjoying lunch and each other's company, the nurses related the following story to Janet. Kay Lynne, a nurse at the hospital where they worked, went book browsing at the landfill. Uh-huh, landfill. She heard they sold books for ten cents a copy, and she was curious what they had. While perusing her choices, Kay Lynne noted a box nearby with the lid at half-mast and pulled back the flaps to look inside. Instead of a stack of books, she was peering into a fuzzy circle of kittens. The newborns weren't even cleaned up well yet.

Kay Lynne asked the manager of the landfill about them. Seems that either the mama cat had confused the landfill for the maternity ward, or her owners had decided to dump the babies. All the manager knew was that they were lying on the ground when he showed up at work. He hadn't decided what he was going to do with them. The nurse knew they initially would take a lot of care and, feeling concerned for their well-being, offered to take them home. The manager sighed with relief.

Once home Kay Lynne realized caring for the newborns was going to be trickier than she had thought. The four kittens were going to need around-the-clock feedings, she was single, and it was time for her shift at the hospital. Kay Lynne warmed some formula and carefully fed each tiny kitten. Then she tucked them in a plastic crate lined with towels and a heating pad and trotted off to work with her new charges.

When she arrived, she proclaimed to her co-workers, "Lookie here what I have." The nurses, all being passionate about cats, squealed with delight and concern over the furry patients. "We'll all help you care for them," the women decided.

They set up a "ward" for the kittens in the nurses' lounge. One nurse appointed herself as responsible for creating the formula and refused to let anyone else even consider taking over the job. She measured out milk and compassion with exquisite care. Each of the other nurses agreed to take a turn administering the eyedropper and the formula.

It worked like a charm, and with the women's nurturing instincts and medical prowess, the tiny kittens responded. One of the little felines was nicknamed Mighty Mouth because he made sure everyone up and down the halls heard him when it was feeding time. (I have relatives like that.) Another kitten relieved himself on a doctor whom the nurses felt was the most deserving person in the hospital for such treatment.

But as those little, fluffy bundles grew, they would scamper into the halls every time the door to the nurses' lounge was opened. The nurses would scurry after them, trying to retrieve them before the mischief-makers landed on some patient's lap.

So the kittens were adopted out. Guess who gave them homes? Yep, the compassionate nurses.

Just think, those little helpless creatures were abandoned at the dump. Okay, landfill, but anyway you gussy it up, it's still garbage. Just take a whiff next time you're book browsing. To be thrown away when you're already helpless leaves you totally vulnerable.

Have you ever been at the mercy of others? Weren't you grateful when someone came along and delivered you?

My friend Terry remembers vividly her rescue when the canoe she and her husband, Ted, were in flipped. They had just turned a bend in the river where the water went from shallow to deep with fast-moving currents, when the canoe rolled. As Terry surfaced in the deep end, she was spitting water and grabbed for a nearby tree limb where she held on for dear life. Ted came up on the opposite side of the boat where the water was shallow and easily waded out of the river. Two men, seeing Terry trying desperately to hold on as the current pulled against her, leapt into the water to rescue her.

Her husband, instead of calling reassuring words to his wife or attempting to rescue her, yelled to the men, "Save the cooler!" Seems lunch had been catapulted into the current and was drifting away while Ted's appetite obviously ate up his good judgment. It's been years since the incident, but the memory of Terry's husband's response still laps on the shores of her mind.

Nope, no nurse's hat for you, Ted.

It's not easy always to be there for folks in the

way they need us to be. I guess that's why nurses go through so much training . . . and why God warns us not to put our confidence in others but instead to place it in Him. Sometimes even those in the medical field can make mistakes.

My mom fell in a restaurant, and as I knelt next to her, I could tell she was in trouble. She had broken her hip and required a full hip replacement. Following her surgery she needed physical therapy. When the therapist came to her room to help her up the first time, I heard the therapist say aloud to herself, "Okay, this gal has had a partial hip replacement," and then she leaned down to lift my mom.

"Just a minute," I interjected. "This lady had a full replacement."

"No, she didn't. I'm the therapist; she had a partial."

"Well, this is my mother, and I don't want you to touch her until you read her chart."

Annoyed, the therapist stomped off and returned a few minutes later agreeing that Mom had had a full replacement, which changed the way the therapist would lift her. While that wasn't a life-threatening mistake, it could have added to Mom's injury and certainly would have caused her pain.

As the psalmist said, "Consider my affliction and deliver me."

Even those of us with the finest training and best intentions need You, O Lord, to deliver us. We are sometimes victims of our own humanity. Thank You that whether we are in over our heads or down and out, that You hear our cries for help and consider us. And when others discard us, you know right where we are, and Your redemptive plan is already in place. Thank You for caring for us in such medicinal ways, and thank You for those You send to aid in our rescue. Prepare us to extend grace when others fail to be there for us and infuse us with courage to face life's inevitable difficulties. Amen.

*Whether the moon is rocking on its
side or in its freckled fullness, causing
shadows to dart among the trees,
I marvel at its beauty.*

Artist's Beret

CONSIDER GOD'S WONDERS

When I consider Your heavens, the work of Your fingers, the moon and the stars, which you have ordained. (Psalm 8:3)

Some of the most exquisite sights I've witnessed have been from the Almighty's canvas: Ebony skies studded with diamond stars; silver-threaded horizons boasting emblazoned suns; purple mountain peaks ensconced in pink clouds. Heaven's displays cause my heart to skip a beat.

I understand when I see such beauty why photographers click hundreds of frames and why artists rush to their drawing boards in hopes of capturing the splendor. I, too, have ached to somehow scoop up, say, a peach sunrise, a double rainbow, or the refraction off a bluebird's wing to slip it into a bottle. Then I could indulgently re-experience the awe again and again.

But breathtaking scenes are vaporous. Occasionally I've called my family to join me in watching a stunning sunset, but by the time they had dashed out, the crimsons and periwinkles had faded into passé grays. And no matter how hard I've tried to describe my sightings in the heavens, the explanations fall short of capturing the experience for others.

So c'mon, grab your artist's beret. We're off to the art room.

Not artistic, you say? Guess again. We have been fashioned by the Master, and He designed us after Himself. Therefore all of us—yes, all—have some strand of artistic flair. So go ahead, tilt that hat, and let's add some color to our lives. I have dibs on fuchsia!

Pablo Picasso said, "Every child is an artist. The problem is how to remain an artist once we grow up."

Since childhood I've enjoyed art supplies: paper, pencils, crayons, paints, chalk, glue, rulers, and erasers. My dilemma was that, once I made my purchases, I was lost as to how to form anything identifiable with them. So for many years the artist inside me lay dormant . . . until I began public speaking.

Selecting the right word to express myself was

like loading a brush with shades of sap green to highlight a landscape. I agree with Mark Twain when he quipped, "The difference between the right word and the almost right word is the difference between lightning and the lightning bug."

I also get a kick out of moving furniture and pictures around my house, creating fresh inside landscapes. The furnishings are my palette and the rooms my canvas. For years I never thought of arranging furniture as an artistic endeavor, but eventually I realized that was the case.

I remember when I was at my friend Ginny's house in California during our nation's 9-11 crisis. Amy, my traveling companion, and I found ourselves grounded for several unexpected days. While we waited for the airlines to start up again, we had some nervous time on our hands. Ginny had mentioned when we arrived that she could use some help rearranging her living room; so one day, while Ginny was running errands and Amy and I were trying not to stress out, we put our hands to the task. The hours flew by as we pushed, pulled, arranged, hammered, and fluffed. We used up some of our tension and exercised our creativity while surprising our hostess. Ginny said her only regret was that we couldn't stay long enough to surprise her in all her rooms.

Art is expressed in more ways than we might have considered. Take organization. I remember visiting a friend who invited me to view her stored canned goods. I thought that was an odd request but one that I could see would please her. When she opened the cellar, the beauty of the display startled me. She had shelf after shelf lined with mason jars filled with peaches, pears, applesauce, green beans, beets, etc. She had aligned them in sections by color, allowing your eye to move from the delicate yellow pears, to the strong orange peaches, to the deep green beans, down to the rich burgundy-red beets. The display was a kaleidoscope of art.

Now hold onto your beret, tilt back your head, and gaze into the heavens. Talk about organization and beauty! The rotation of the sun, seasons, and solar system gives us a personal sense of placement and predictability, both of which add to our feeling safe. We like to know we have a particular spot on planet Earth that's ours, that some semblance of order exists in this place, and that we have enough daily sameness to feel anchored.

I look forward to evening inspections of

heaven's canopy, as I search for starry dippers and visually measure the moon. Whether the moon is rocking on its side or in its freckled fullness, causing shadows to dart among the trees, I marvel at its beauty. When I scan the firmament, I agree with the old astronomer who said, "I love the stars too much to be afraid of the night."

Even more than the stars, I love the fingers that formed them, the One whose hands guide us through our darkest nights.

Art for me is a meeting of the mind and heart, capturing elements of beauty, tragedy, and mystery. Fine art is not only carefully executed strokes on a page but also any creative endeavor done with principled passion.

If you're like me, as a child, you wanted to step inside a storybook to live in a castle or to own a white stallion or to sail to a faraway land. Well, just think, God allows us daily to step onto His canvas where we are surrounded by vibrant trees, fragrant flowers, and expansive skies; where leaves turn crimson, clouds saunter, and stars actually leave trails of glittering dust. When I consider God's handiwork, I'm inspired and want to help color my world.

I christened a room in my home my Art Room. There I wrap gifts, design cards, work on notebooks, and read stories to my grandson, Justin. My artist friend Carol painted on one of the walls a garden with paths, a trellis, and birds. The room is an inviting respite.

Do you have a space of your own? One where you can create? It doesn't have to be elaborate. Why, it doesn't have to be a room. It could be a cozy chair, a closet, a porch swing, or a designated corner. There you could knit a sweater, write encouraging notes to your friends, journal, sketch, design your next garden, plan a menu, set your creative priorities, or pray. When we consider the beauty found in the heavens, the sky becomes the limit for our personal endeavors.

But for me to get my beret on straight, I first had to rearrange my thinking. In the past I had limited my artistic endeavors because I didn't want my creative expression to be done incorrectly or to look foolish. I started to turn the corner when I concentrated more on who God was and less on who I wasn't. The more I investigated God's love through the Scriptures the more I relaxed; the safety of His love untied the knot of anxiety and perfectionism within me.

Today, when I consider the heavens, I'm reminded that God ordained this splendor for us. That makes me want to toss my beret toward the heavens with a shout! Come, join me.

Then we'll fetch our berets, pull them back on, and enter our worlds with holy flair.

*The Gardener is near, and He will
use our times, trials, temptations,
and tears to cause us to bloom.*

Gardening Hat

CONSIDER HOW YOUR SPIRITUAL GARDEN GROWS

Consider the lilies, how they grow. (Luke 12:27)

My garden hat is off to the female population. I'm so impressed with all we do and how we do it. That isn't to suggest that I wouldn't tip my hat for the men as well, but I've just come from a Women of Faith conference so the fragrance of women's courage is fresh on my mind. The stories I heard from women who attended the conference reminded me how tough some women have it and how they have weathered megaobstacles with grace and integrity.

Their fortitude reminds me of the bulbs I planted in my yard last fall. They lay dormant through the bitter winter, but then in the spring they began the arduous journey of pushing up life through the crusty earth while sending stabilizing roots into the soil. And just when we wonder if Old Man Winter will ever pack up and leave town, we see the green leaves of promise and then the bursting buds of color that dazzle us with hope.

Some of my favorite bulb flowers are lilies, especially the summer daylilies. I love the way they sway in the wind and brighten corners. They are willowy and feminine, yet they are hardy. You can shovel them up and replant them almost anywhere, and they seem determined to survive and even thrive. And they cluster with other lilies, making quite a show on roadsides, in fields, and in yards.

Do you feel rooted, watered, and ready for whatever weather comes your way?

One winsome lily of a gal, Betsy, sped up to my book table at a Women of Faith conference riding a Rascal (three-wheeled cart). A multiple sclerosis and cancer survivor, she was determined not to allow her health challenges to squelch her determination to enter into the thick of life.

Betsy and a friend asked to have individual pictures taken with me, to which I joyfully agreed. Betsy swung her legs around and rose to a standing position, which I could see wasn't easy for her. I stepped in close to Betsy, slipping my hand around her back to steady her, and I whispered, "I don't want you to fall." To which she countered, "If I do, then I'll just get back up again."

I could tell by her spunk that Betsy, like daylilies beaten down after a storm, was experienced at "getting back up again." The biting winds of adversity had only rooted her courage. Betsy's girlfriend asked Betsy if she would take a picture of us, which surprised me because the multiple sclerosis had compromised Betsy's hands and left her with fierce tremors. But with true grit birthed in the winter of her pain, Betsy gripped the camera and brought it to her face. With the camera shaking badly, it took a few moments for her to find us through the viewer, but Betsy did it. Her actions dazzled me with hope. I wanted to shout, celebrate, weep, and repent.

You see, I have to confess that, after being around Betsy and others like her, I realized how tart I become when inconvenienced. It doesn't take much of a breeze to topple me. I want to believe that, if called upon to be a heroine, I would rise to the occasion like Betsy. But experience has proven me feeble.

I tend to bloom best on sunny days—times when I have eight to nine hours sleep per night, a moderate diet, balanced portions of work and play, and harmony within my relationships. Yeah, like all that's going to happen at the same time.

Now that I've advanced into life's autumn season (I'm knee-deep in age), I don't sleep well or long. That annoys me. And soon I annoy others with my edgy responses. To entertain myself when I'm up too late and then back up too early, I snack too often. That's too many too's. As for balance, I feel as if my schedule is a gyrating seesaw, making it difficult to maintain equilibrium.

What has helped me to grow the most through this blustery season is adjusting my mental attitude. Mind-checks are a must for me so I don't slide back into unhealthy habits. One thing I've learned is that I don't need as much sleep as I'd like to have, but I do need to be grateful for what I get. Otherwise I can talk myself right into an exhausted heap. Owning my edginess instead of justifying my reactive behavior has helped to improve my disposition. Also, thinking before I nibble a crater the size of Kansas through the middle of a coffee cake helps. And last, pacing my activities as best I can, even during life's unavoidable frenetic times.

Ten-minute catnaps can be restorative, I've

found. Next time you have a few extra moments, slip a couple of cucumber slices over your eyes, give yourself ten quiet minutes, and voila, you'll feel like a salad. Only kidding. You'll feel refreshed, and your eyes will look more rested.

Growth and change are synonymous. Perhaps you're in the midst of change, and it feels threatening. That's often the initial signal that alerts us to a season of growth. The rumble of thunder in the distance and the soil of struggle form the environment that nurtures us and gives us Easter lily potential.

Did you know the majority (more than 80 percent) of Easter lilies, our resurrection flower, are grown in one strip of land out west? Seems the temperature, soil, sunshine, and rainfall in that area are exactly what they need to thrive.

As I've wondered if my roots might be too close to the surface, I'm grateful to know that our feebleness qualifies us for God's strength. When we experience that strengthening, our character and resolve deepen. Whew!

The Lord knows the difficulty factor in our strip of land and will use it to call forth new life within us. He will deepen our faith, cultivate our character, and water our parched hearts. We are resurrection people because of Jesus. So fear not, gardening buddies; instead consider this: The Gardener is near, and He will use our times, trials, temptations, and tears to cause us to bloom.

O Lord of the fallen flower,
Lifter of the storm tossed bloom,
Enter my heart's bowed garden
And make for yourself room.

Cultivate my hardness,
Reign new life into me
Shower me with mercy drops
Till I rise and bloom for Thee.

       —Patsy

I'm mentally jiggly, and like a butterfly,
my thoughts can flutter off capriciously.

Thinking Cap

CONSIDER YOUR
THOUGHT LIFE

Consider my meditation. (Psalm 5:1)

"Use your head for something other than a hat rack," my dad would quip when I wasn't making sense, which as a kid was frequently. His advice still makes me giggle.

I was a child given to whimsy, and as I grew into adulthood, the temptation never left me. I often need rocks in my pockets to keep my feet on the ground lest I fly off on a playful endeavor when I should be toeing the mark. Even as I write, I keep thinking how much fun it would be to dash into our quaint town and visit the shops or dial a friend for a chatty update.

I'm mentally jiggly, and like a butterfly, my thoughts can flutter off capriciously. Years ago I realized that, if I didn't net in my flyaway thoughts, I would accomplish very little, learn less, and lead a disconnected lifestyle. My longing then was to become mentally focused, emotionally balanced, and spiritually fit. Those goals remain at the top of my list, but quite honestly, some seasons I do better than others.

So how does one begin to connect the dots and capture runaway thoughts? It's like lassoing a lizard—it takes lots of practice. In fact, you may want to grab your thinking cap for this chapter and join me in evaluating the contents of our thought life. For if we are going to pray like the psalmist, "Consider my meditation," we will need to examine what's on our minds.

How would you answer the following?

Most of my thoughts in a day are about _____(me, coworkers, me, sweetheart, me, children, me, job, me, problems).

My thoughts are generally _____ (wholesome, negative, uplifting, critical).

My mind is too _____ (busy, slow, brooding, tired, repetitive, bored).

If you're like me, your answer could be "all of the above," depending on the day, season, and circumstances. Our minds are constantly evaluating our surroundings, feeding us information, monitoring our bodies, and allowing us to process thoughts. Brains are amazing, active, imaginative, and hungry.

Hungry?

I've found the more I nurture my thought life the healthier it seems to be. The Old Testament prophet Jeremiah said, "Your words were found, and I ate them, and Your word was to me the joy and rejoicing of my heart" (Jeremiah 15:16).

I don't think Jeremiah fricasseed a scroll and chowed down, but I do believe he mentally feasted on the truth. He devoured the life-giving understanding of who God is, and the very thought filled him with delicious joy.

At times my mind breeds dismal thoughts, conjures up negative ideas, and indulges unhealthy musings. I need to swing open the windows and doors of my thought life and air it out.

I'm not always sure what brings about this stagnant thinking. I just know that, if I don't deal with it, my emotions, energy, health, and relationships are all infected. But airing out isn't enough; I also have to shore up my thoughts by filling my mind with good stuff.

Still have your thinking cap secured? Let's consider a menu that will feed our minds, give us food for our faith, nurture our confidence, strengthen our relationships, and increase our joy.

Literature. Books have played an important part of restructuring my thoughts. They help me to see how others overcame obstacles and faced devastation whether in a biography or a well-penned novel by a seasoned journeyer.

How long has it been since you've read a classic? Why not sink into your favorite chair with a copy of Hannah Hurnard's allegory, *Hinds Feet on High Places.* Journey with Much Afraid to the high places and be reminded of God's constancy in your life. Or have you traveled with *Christy* by Catherine Marshall into the Appalachian coves of South Carolina? There young Christy learns to trust God in the midst of feuds, prejudices, and superstitions. The story recounts the struggles of the human heart.

When my mind is too muddled or harried with pressure, I'll listen to a book on tape. It can be a pleasant treat—actually quite nurturing—to have someone read to you.

Music. "Music is the language of holy joy," said John Wesley. I would agree, for it can lead you into the presence of the Joy Giver and cause your heart to dance. I find music is motivational too. Imagine sitting still through "When the Saints Go Marching In." I don't think it can be done. Even glued to a pew, my feet are two-stepping. I remember years ago at my home church on Father's Day the men would march up onto the platform singing that "holy joy" song, and it would be all I could do not to race down the aisle to join them.

Music also soothes, which is why mamas whisper lullabies to their babies, sweethearts croon love songs to each other, and strains of Beethoven waft through elevators, waiting rooms, and lobbies. Even Old Testament King Saul called for David to play music to soothe his distraught nerves. When my hubby and I feel jangled, we bask in the tenor sunshine of Andrea Bocelli. Selections like "*Un Canto,*" "*Dí tu se fedele,*" and "The Prayer" (a duet with Celine Dion) make us call out, "*Bella!*"

Choosing wholesome music and books helps to create a favorable atmosphere for our thought life. It's like planting seeds as we make deliberate choices about what enters our minds. The crop we reap with wise mind-fodder is fruitful thoughts, ones that grow the soul.

Scripture. God's Word has brought me through dark years by shedding stepping-stone pools of light that directed me out of the labyrinth of depression, loss, and fear. It also guided me out of an overdose of myself. I had dined on an exaggerated menu of me, me, me, and quite honestly, it had become nauseating.

What did I want?

What did I think?

How did I feel?

Those thoughts dominated my mind, and as important as those questions are to answer, when that's all we think about, it's time to step out of ourselves and into a larger world. Life is not just about us . . . fortunately.

Read afresh one of the Gospels and note the time Jesus took for Himself and then compare the countless times He invested in others. We are instructed to become like Him, to think like He thought, selflessly.

Of all outside influences, Scripture has had the most profound impact on my mind and emotions. From the pages of Holy Writ the Spirit of God has pressed truth, comfort, conviction, and principles into my understanding. In those pages my thinking cap is put to its best use, as I ponder His high ways, ways that aren't naturally mine. Then I feel confident to pray, "Dear Lord, consider my meditation."

God is good. That truth tucked up
under our shower caps will help
us to bear up under wrenching
winds and pelting rains.

~ Shower Cap ~

CONSIDER THE STORMY
SEASON

*Consider . . . surely God has appointed the one [day of
prosperity] as well as the other [day of adversity].*
(Ecclesiastes 7:13–14)

I have quite a stack of shower caps littering my
bathroom shelves that I've collected from my
frequent stays in hotels. You wouldn't want to get
caught wearing one of these in a rainstorm since
they're so skimpy. And I might add they're far
from a fashion statement . . . unlike my rubber
ducky shower cap.

My cap isn't a statement; it's a proclamation.
It's full of vibrant colors and includes the image of
a pudgy yellow duck in a tub—and since it's about
the thickness of a rain barrel, it could withstand a
cloudburst. (I probably wouldn't, but after the

storm they would find my duck still quacking.)
Now you probably wouldn't want to wear my cap
to, say, church, but you might pack it in your gym
bag for a few giggles at sauna time.

Actually, when you consider life, it makes sense
to tuck a few shower caps in one's pocket. We
never know when we might run into squalls, and
umbrellas can be so cumbersome.

My cousin Julya understands unexpected show-
ers. She and her husband, Richard, own a forty-
two-foot DeFever 40, which is a trawler (fishing
vessel) that putters about at ten knots top speed.
The couple has been traveling by waterways for
quite sometime. Their last boating venture lasted
for ten months. Now that's a trip. With the excep-
tion of Women of Faith conferences, my last trip
was over the footstool on my way to bed and lasted
about three and a half spectacular seconds.

At one point in Julya and Richard's latest journey, they found themselves in a spectacular and
dangerous storm. They could see the lightning
strikes ripping at the water all around them; so
they moved their vessel in close to the shore for
some refuge from the winds, waves, and rain, and
then the couple hung on for dear life. Strapped

into their life jackets, they could smell the ozone, and the radical shift in atmospheric pressure caused their hair to stand on end. Afterward they learned that tornados had rampaged across the land on both sides of them. Call me quacked up, but this landlubber is sticking to her bathtub and shower cap.

The weather warnings didn't clear for Julya even after the clouds blew by and the waters stilled. After arriving at her home harbor, she stepped ashore to receive the results of her yearly health report. Julya had breast cancer.

One thing about violent storms, they deepen your prayer life. Just ask Julya. Or Vivian . . .

Viv and I have been heart sisters for many years and live only a few blocks apart. Because of our busy lives, months can pass before we catch up. Lately though, we've been talking weekly because one adversity after another has rained down on Viv's life.

For one thing, Vivian is moving. Only those who have remained anchored for many years will think this isn't a biggie. But trust me, I've relocated more than thirty times during my forty-year marriage, and moving is stormy weather for most of us,

U-Haul or not, y'all. The dismantling of belongings is an emotional thunderstorm, and I'm sure Viv will experience loud rumblings as she packs up the twenty years of debris—I mean, belongings—that have stockpiled.

Add to moving, Viv's son Blake, his three children, and their high-strung Russian wolfhound, Jujubee, moved in a few weeks back. Blake's wife flew to Europe to settle her grandmother's estate and will be gone for almost two months. Viv had agreed in quieter times that she would keep the family and be the babysitter-driver-cook while Blake worked.

Oh, did I mention, the day after her daughter-in-law left, Viv's husband, William, tripped over a skateboard sustaining a compound fracture? It required several surgeries before the doctors bolted his bones back together. William's recuperation (foot in air) and therapy (uh-huh, Viv shuttles him back and forth) will keep him out of the workforce and without a paycheck for months.

During William's elderly father's chemotherapy, he is staying in the last vacant corner of Viv's home. So Viv once again became the taxi for another member of her family. This gal doesn't need a shower cap; she needs a waterproof chauffeur's license.

When her father-in-law wants Viv to wait on him, he raps his cane on the floor until the lamps in the house jiggle. He feels that's kinder than yelling.

For some reason Vivian has hives.

These thunderous situations, dear friends, are more than a storm; they are a typhoon!

It reminds me of that grand old quip, "When it rains it pours." Or what about, "Life ain't no ride on no pink duck." (Hmm, that's okay. My yellow ducky would have clashed with that pink fowl anyway.) Scripture puts it this way, "Man is born to trouble as surely as sparks fly upward" (Job 5:7 NIV). To that Viv would offer a resounding "amen."

If you could meet them for lunch, here's what Julya and Vivian would tell you over a Caesar salad: Life is treacherous, and life is tremendous. We all know this, but here is the clincher: The stabilizing truth that acts as the cohesive to hold us together is that, through all of life's weather patterns, God is good. That truth tucked up under our shower caps will help us to bear up under wrenching winds and pelting rains. Knowing in our noggin that God is good liberates us from despair and comforts us with hope. When we know we can trust His redeeming hand, then even the category-five storms don't mentally blow us away.

Julya told me when they sailed down to Marathon and Boot Key, Florida, they ran into seventy-five-mile-per-hour winds. They dragged three anchors until they could tie off at a pump station and wait for things to settle down.

I've had a few three-anchor seasons myself. How about you? I tell you what, let's tie off at God's pump station, His Word, and renew our minds. Then, when we settle down into His good-ness, we'll cast off again full sail. Don't forget your shower cap.

P.S. Julya's surgery was a success, and she didn't have to go through prolonged treatments because all the lymph nodes were clear. Soon she'll be charging through the blue waters again.

Vivian and her family gradually are returning to a less frayed existence. William's foot has healed in record time. Business details came together quickly for their daughter-in-law, and she returned three weeks early.

Jujubee the wolfhound is another story. Seems she and the collie down the street, Woof-Woof, hit it off. Uh-oh, those pups are going to need a hair-dresser.

Ah, but Viv's father-in-law's cane tapping has been replaced with the sound of a melodic bell presented to him by Viv. And yippee, the hives are gone.

Walking the two-thousand-mile Oregon Trail would have been out of the question for me unless I could have tailed behind the wagon train in my PT Cruiser.

~ Bonnet ~

CONSIDER THE PAST—AND
THE FUTURE

Consider the years of many generations.
(Deuteronomy 32:7)

Any scary relatives in your past?

A few years back, I had to take down an old family picture I had hanging in a stairwell because it frightened my overnight guests and their children. Actually, I'm not even sure who the fellow was, but I think he might have been a great-great-grandfather. I named him Grumpy. Regardless of his identity, he now resides in my storage room overseeing my Christmas decorations. Sorry, Grandpa Grumpy.

Photographs of folks from bygone years presented them as stern. Of course, times were tough and work rugged, so I guess we shouldn't be surprised by the dour looks.

When I was a youngster, I thought I would have loved to live in the days of the wagon trains. I romanticized the pioneers' journeys and lifestyle, believing waterfalls, good-looking cowboys with neck scarves, and starlit campfires awaited them at every bend.

But a dip into history quickly sets the record straight. Why, those bonnet-clad ladies worked like mules (who do you think split the wood for the fire?), and they had minimal comforts or conveniences (and, honey, those cowboys seldom bathed).

Okay, I'll admit I'm rather fond of my dishwasher and trash compactor, not to mention my whirlpool tub. And my idea of a long walk is a lap around my neighborhood—if it's not too hot, cold, wet, or windy. So walking the two-thousand-mile Oregon Trail would have been out of the question for me unless I could have tailed the wagon train in my PT Cruiser. But I'm not certain how far it would have gone fueled by buffalo chips. Besides, if I endured such a hard trek— wrought with flooded rivers, contaminated water holes, outbreaks of cholera, and constant accidents—I would want my final destination to be a spa, not an undeveloped frontier I had to forge a living from. This means no Nordstrom or Starbucks! Where did they get their Ralph Laurens and mocha lattes?

Many of those frontier folks initially built homes made of sod. Isn't that chunks of dirt? Even though those chunks kept you cool in the summer and warm in the winter, mice and rats (eek!) lived in the sod. And snakes and gophers liked to gnaw their way through the sod to share in tea and flap-jacks. Okay, that does it. I'm staying right where I am, thank you.

Those cloistered-looking bonnets the women wore were, by the sounds of it, the only shady refuge the womenfolk had in a day. No wonder the brims were so deep. Yes, nothing like a history lesson to give one a reality check.

Hey, grab a bonnet—just for this chapter, I promise—and let's contemplate some past gener-ations of women to collect their wisdom for us today. Women like . . .

Hannah. An Old Testament gal, Hannah was under constant family ridicule, but she used her humiliation and pain to deepen her prayer life.

Hannah's response to her distress was to kneel in Jehovah's presence, crying out for help. She longed to be a mom not only because she wanted a baby but also because motherhood would solidify her role in the ranks of her husband's wives. But Hannah was judged by others and looked down on because of her barren womb. Her personal pain was so overwhelming that, as she knelt at the altar to agonize before the Lord God, a priest observed her distraught behavior and decided Hannah was drunk.

Have you ever been drunk with heartbreak?

I remember staggering about when word came that my brother, Don, who was thirty-eight years old, had died from injuries following a car accident. I felt my loss, the loss for my parents of their only son, and the loss for Don's six children. Reeling, I reached out to a friend who steadied my thoughts with Scripture and prayed for my loved ones and me. While my friend was supportive, it was God's presence and the truth of His Word that penetrated my pain and comforted my agonized mind. I understood Hannah's need to cry out to the only One who could meet her in the midst of her travail.

Miriam. Miriam, Moses' sister, was known among their people for her singing, wisdom, and leadership, but then she nitpicked and usurped her brother's authority. Miriam had, in her old age, developed a critical spirit. She became a rebel, an outcast, and a leper.

Miriam's behavior makes me cry, "Ouch!" I can so easily think I know more than I do and become so self-certain that I forget who is in charge of all that concerns me. Not to mention my tendency to pass judgment on others.

What makes folks critical? Resentment? Insecurity? Arrogance? Jealousy? Or perhaps all of the above.

I'm thankful to say that, after Miriam's humiliation and isolation, she was restored back to her people. Her critical attitude cost her a lot (health, position, and reputation), and that sort of attitude is costly to us as well. We won't get leprosy from it, but I guarantee it affects our well-being and atrophies our spirit. It also strains relationships with others, which leaves us often feeling misunderstood and lonely.

Who deliberately wants to be around someone who is critical? I don't see any raised hands out there. A critical spirit is constricting, cruel, and caustic. I know. Keep this under your bonnet, but

I've repeatedly had to present my own sharp tongue and stubborn nature to the Lord. I've also noticed that being critical of others is as habit-forming as nicotine and caffeine. (I've been addicted to those as well.) And anything that rules us (aside from the lordship of Christ) tends to stifle the music in our hearts. When I'm critical, I've found that's often a warning that I'm too busy, too tired, and too self-absorbed.

So how can we have a melody restored?

1. Ask the Lord to give us a new song, a toe-tapping song of praise.

2. Practice praising others, not the empty words of someone trying too hard to make restitution but sincere words of truth so that they fit into the hearer's heart.

3. When we mess up, take responsibility for our harshness as soon as possible. This was a formidable step for me because taking responsibility squashes pride (ouch) and reveals character (oh, my). But it also aids in breaking the habit (yeah!).

I can see why we're instructed to investigate past generations. It causes us to consider how those who have trod the path before us have handled heartbreaks and hardships.

BONNET

Well, I promised that you only had to wear the bonnet for this chapter, but you might want to slip it on from time to time on your own. The next time you pass a mirror and the reflection looks like Grandpa Grumpy, grab your bonnet and head for the Scriptures. While we aren't to live in yesterday, we're encouraged to visit there. It can be a place of refuge and a way to learn a fresh chorus of praise. All of which prepares us to slip into the future with our hearts secure in whose we are and how we're to behave.

*Ravens are scavenger birds,
the pirates of the air,
out looking for a meal.*

❧ Pirate's Hat ❧

CONSIDER GOD'S CARE

Consider the ravens. (Luke 12:24)

You're not going to believe this, but honest, this story is true. (I promise you my prize, 1940s Shirley Temple paper dolls if it isn't!) A relative of my friend Bev unexpectedly moved into Bev's home for a lengthy stay.

Okay, that's disruptive, but not unbelievable, you say? Just wait.

This relative, whom we'll call Gwenda, came with baggage. Not just with luggage but with her pets in tow. Yes, pets, plural. A dog, Bertha, dubbed for her gargantuan size and a wiry chicken named Weezer.

Don't check your hearing aid; you heard right, a cotton-pickin' chicken. Now I have a lot of friends who own pet birds, but a chicken!? Just hearing that a fowl moved into Bev's house ruffled my feathers.

Fortunately, Weezer showed up in a cage. I know this because Bev decided shortly after Weezer's arrival to change the newspapers in the tray (for obvious reasons). Bev grabbed up the comic strips and quickly lined the bottom of the cage, thinking what a sacrificial effort she was making. A little while later Gwenda strolled by, spotted the comics, and hit the roof. Seems Weezer doesn't have a sense of humor because she only likes the black and white sections of the newspaper. No, I'm not making this up. The funnies are not funny to Weezer.

So Bev pulled out the "Family Circus" and replaced it with the obituaries. Weezer nestled right in.

And get this: Weezer loves lettuce, but it has to be heated first. I wonder how Gwenda figured that out. Maybe Weezer pecked out a message like Morse code. "Gwenda, for heaven's sake, heat the lettuce!"

Anyway, Gwenda frequents Bev's already congested kitchen, skillet in hand, sautéing Weezer's gourmet meals. (I have a feeling the hostess would like to sauté . . . well, never mind.) Weezer is no dumb cluck. This chick knows which side her lettuce is heated on.

Speaking of heat, Weezer's home state of Florida, known for its warm days, annoys Weezer's sensitivities; so Gwenda keeps a fan running for her chickette. I can hear Weezer now: "A little to the right . . . now a little to the left . . . ahh, that's better." Talk about ruffled feathers. Can you picture a fanned chicken—feathers parted, head plastered against the bars, wings pulsating in time to the whir.

If you're thinking about adopting the Weezer clan, know that your electric bill will grow. Seems when you go out for the evening, Weezer gets scared if left in the dark, so you'll need to leave on the lights.

And if you're thinking it won't matter, then know that big Bertha becomes frantic when her chicken friend isn't happy and tends to leave little droplets around the house. Actually, nothing big Bertha leaves could be described as little. (Did I mention Bertha would only drink her water from a Starbucks coffee mug?)

Life is definitely funnier than fiction. And a neurotic chicken makes me cluck. Of course, I can guffaw because Weezer is hundreds of miles away from me. If this group were my houseguests, why, the solution seems simple. I'd send Weezer, Bertha, and their keeper to a faraway farm, perhaps to a funny farm. There Weezer could possibly develop a sense of humor. Then I'd call Kentucky Fried Chicken; that way Weezer could have a last laugh. Run, chicken, run!

Okay, okay, I wouldn't call the Colonel, but golly, girls, that chick has no right to come in and take over Bev's home like, well, like a pirate or something.

Have you ever had anyone enter your life and just take over? Maybe, like Weezer, the intruder's demands pressured you into making more adjustments than you ever meant to. Perhaps you started off with a gesture of kindness, like Bev's, and ended up with the guest taking over your personal space and freedoms.

Come to think of it, most of us have had people take advantage of our generosity and our hospitality. In fact, we may have even been the one at some point doing the pirating of someone else's ship.

I confess, when my husband and I were young marrieds and not terribly mature but terribly broke, we lived with my parents several times. Stuffing our belongings throughout their home, we settled in and reveled in Mom's home cooking.

My parents eventually moved into a mobile home. Now I wonder if we unknowingly nudged them toward a small nest so they could limit their visitor potential. I wouldn't have blamed them. It's hard to live with people—even loved ones without chickens. (Although my sister lived with my folks at that time, and she had a parrot that chomped a hole in Mom's rattan chair and nibbled the wooden shade off the window.)

When I married Les, even as a teenager, I found it frustrating to have to adapt to his expectations. Get this, girls, my pirate-hubby thought I wanted to meet all his needs. Cackle, cackle. He certainly hadn't read the same books I had in which the prince scoops up the princess and takes her home to the palace (maids, serfs, etc.) to meet all her needs. Les's version must have read: The pirate drags (figuratively) the princess around the ship and tells her to swab the decks. So we rode a rocky boat, with our swords drawn, as we battled for control.

And control really is a big part of the issue, whether a couple is battling each other's boundaries or houseguests can't remember it's not their house. Wheedling our way into someone's home and then not respecting their space is treason on the high seas, punishable by walking the plank. So if you're the least bit chicken . . .

Really, though, for those of us being pirated around by outsiders or insiders, we need to sit down and do some serious negotiating.

And, girls, I don't encourage us to sport the featured hat in this chapter. Enough pirates are roaming around in the world without our adding to the headcount. And we probably won't want to go out and buy a Weezer, but we may want to consider the ravens . . . oh, not for purchase, but for winged thoughts to ponder.

Ravens are scavenger birds, the pirates of the air, out looking for a meal. But here's the impressive part: God provides it. Sometimes, not always, but sometimes, those we take in are our guests by God's design. He is using us and them for more reasons than we understand. That's where inconvenience becomes relinquishment, and relinquishment leads to a more expansive heart for us all.

So if Aunt Gwenda knocks with Bertha at her side and Weezer tucked under her arm, before we send them off to the farm, realize they may be God's ravens.

Before Les's head hits the pillow, nocturnal growls are puffing through his flared nostrils and sputtering lips—at least a 4.6 on the Richter scale.

~ Sleeping Cap ~

CONSIDER SLUMBERING
SOUNDLY

Consider and hear me, O LORD my God; enlighten my eyes,
lest I sleep the sleep of death. (Psalm 13:3)

Have you ever been so frustrated that you exclaimed, "I could just lie down right here and die"? I have. Of course I didn't mean it. That was just the most startling thing I could say at that moment, and I wanted somebody to understand I was unraveling. I've always been a bit of a drama queen.

To tell you the truth, my sense of drama increases at night. I'm not sure what that's about, but the nighttime hours can seem longer, sadder, scarier, and lonelier than daytime hours. At times, I've just wanted to pull my sleeping cap down over my eyes, skip the night, and leap into morning.

What keeps you awake? Have you noticed noises are amplified by darkness? Sounds like dripping faucets, clicking furnaces, tingling hot water heaters, gusts of wind, floor squeaks, commode flushes, clocks ticking, and tree branches scratching. Ever snort and wake yourself up? Now that's startling.

For some reason my hearing is heightened at night, causing me to detect a housefly's footsteps as he tiptoes his way across my bathroom mirror. And many a night a fly's confounded buzzing has drawn me out of bed with magazine in hand, rolled, and ready to rap some sense into his knobby little head.

But it's the unfamiliar midnight noises that bug me the most.

"Les, Les. Hey, Les."

"Wh-what?"

"Do you hear that?"

"What?"

"That."

"No."

"Well, wake up and listen!"

"Patsy, Patsy. Hey, Patsy."

"What?"

"Go to sleep!"

Oh, sure. Easy for him to say. Before Les's head

hits the pillow, nocturnal growls are puffing through his flared nostrils and sputtering lips—at least a 4.6 on the Richter scale.

I'm not a sheep counter. I've never been good at math. Besides, if I give my brain too much to do in the evening, I end up keeping myself awake with the racket. I hate to admit this, but sometimes my own wordy prayers cure my sleeplessness. Now, if I bore myself to sleep with my many words, how must God feel about my prattle?

Sometimes reading at bedtime can lull me to sleep. That string of words forming into lettered waves helps to rock the tension out of my tangled thoughts and quiet my hyper-hearing. And while it might not be the greatest book endorsement, reading has been a successful way for me to get some shuteye.

While my hearing refines after dusk, my eyesight diminishes. Yep, the lights really go out. This can cause me to see things that aren't there. In fact, just the other evening I flew into my home airport at midnight. As my husband, my son, and I drove away from the terminal and circled the airport acreage, I spotted red, white, and green illuminated Christmas trees. Hundreds of them.

"Look! Oh, wow!" I exclaimed as I pointed out

into the field. I was impressed some business had invested so much for the holidays.

"What?" Les and Jason asked, peering into the night.

"The trees, all those Christmas trees lit up." I felt a tad annoyed that these guys weren't more observant. Men often don't seem to be as aware of their surroundings as we gals are.

Craning their necks first toward the field and then back toward me, I could tell by their arched eyebrows that they weren't getting it. Les looked at something shiny in the folds of my lap. "Put on your glasses," he patronized.

I fumbled for my glasses, knowing it wasn't going to make a whit of difference. But when I raised my spectacles to look through them, all the sparkling trees came into focus and were transformed into hundreds of individual landing lights on the runways. I would have sworn they were Christmas trees. Good thing I'm not a pilot, or in my attempt to spare the holiday wonderland, we would have landed at the ticket counter or, worse yet, the security checkpoint.

So if I can't see the trees for the forest, wait, or is that the forest for the trees . . . Anyway, if I don't see well, I over-hear, which leaves me sleepless in Michigan, and I prattle in prayer. Golly, it makes me want to lie down right here and die.

I understand why the psalmist cried out to the Lord so frequently. We are needy people. I know, I know I lumped you in with me, but I don't like to feel alone in my stuff. Besides, I'm sure if you thought about it, you've had nights in which you wrestled with the sheets in an attempt to get a few winks, right? And times when you thought things were one way only to find out they were definitely another way, correct? Have you ever said more than was necessary? Perhaps? Once? Or upon hearing a night noise, did you think it to be a mouse? Or a monster? If so, may I say, "Hello, Sister Stocking Cap!"

The Lord has given those of us who are fretters some prescriptions and promises that will help to soothe our ruffled minds in our darkest nights. Pause and consider these:

"I lay down and slept; I awoke, for the LORD sustained me" (Psalm 3:5).

"Meditate within your heart on your bed, and be still" (Psalm 4:4).

"I will both lie down in peace, and sleep; for

You alone, O LORD, make me dwell in safety" (Psalm 4:8).

"When you lie down, you will not be afraid; yes, you will lie down and your sleep will be sweet" (Proverbs 3:24).

Relinquishing fearful thoughts and worrisome projections helps to safeguard our minds and allows us to nestle a little deeper into our stocking caps. But how can we give up the things that cause us the most grief and stress when they stomp around in the night kicking up tension? From what I can tell, purposefully trusting the One who has our best interest in mind. While we can't imagine how things can work out, the Lord is moving on our behalf to bring about resolution to the matter. It's amazing, but most of what we fuss and fume over never happens. So it only makes sense to give up a habit like worry, which robs us of peace, and to replace it with a growing confidence that He who has begun a good work in us will bring it to completion.

Some years ago I wrote a stocking cap reminder to myself. Maybe it will encourage you. "Our Shepherd never slumbers so sleep, sheep."

I now realize I wasn't in need of new headgear but of new gear for my head—a new way of thinking.

Crowning Moment

What's a house without a roof? What's a present without a ribbon? What's a queen without a crown? And, girlfriends, what's a head without a hat?

While sometimes I can look silly wearing a hat, I also figure hats can make me appear taller than my sixty-inch height, which could use a boost (and hats are easier to transport than ladders). Besides, I think hats help to hold brain cells in place—I seem to have misplaced a slew of them during hatless moments. And hats help to keep my locks incognito on bad hair days.

Of course, hats can also create bad hair days. More than once I've removed a baseball cap only to unveil a giant mushroom woven out of my squashed hair. Despite the fungal appearance, on cold days headgear sure keeps me warmer. I'm from the frosty Midwest, and I've learned that most of our body heat escapes out the tops of our heads, which gives added dynamics to the phrase "put a lid on it."

But of far greater importance than what sits atop our heads is what's inside them. As a former agoraphobic (one who is emotionally and physically housebound), I now realize I wasn't in need of new headgear but of new gear for my head—a new way of thinking. That began as I learned to line up my thoughts with God's truth. So much of my thinking had been distorted by my woundedness and my willfulness. Through His Word God offered me healing for my wounds, and His bottom-line principles and forgiveness caused my stubborn will to relax. As I set my cap toward Jesus, my head and my heart began to look up.

Stop and think about the last time you were in the pits. (We all make pit stops along life's journey.) What helped you climb out? A person? A kindness? A medication? A book? A break? Or perhaps a Scripture?

One of my favorite pit verses is Psalm 40:2–3.

It is chock-full of victory and hope. "He also brought me up out of a horrible pit, out of the miry clay, and set my feet upon a rock, and established my steps. He has put a new song in my mouth—praise to our God."

David had known the darkness of disappointment, depression, and despair; yet he climbed out of those pits with God's help. I love the word pictures of the rock-solid place to stand, the steadfast steps because of God's unchanging ways, and the notable vocal transformation.

Isn't that true? When we think differently, we sound differently. I know I do.

Last week I was feeling down over some disappointing news, and you could hear it in my negative conversations and see it in my tension-producing attitudes. When a family member challenged me on my behavior, I backpedaled and asked the Lord for a rock on which to set my shaky emotions and a song for my gnarly disposition. I began reciting my verse from the Psalms as a reminder of God's willingness to rescue me from a pit, even the pit of self-absorption.

As I set my mind (much like I would set my alarm clock, deliberately and specifically), I then was able to move through my disappointment. I reminded myself that Jesus continues to be a redeemer, and He could use my disappointing situation for purposes beyond my understanding. Also, I realized that this letdown was a mere pebble in my life-road, and I didn't have to allow it to trip me up. Nor did I need to add to its effect by piling on boulders of bleakness.

Now if only I could safety-pin those truths to my brain. Thinking God's way is not effortless for me. I have to work at it. Memorization of God's Word helps to shore up my thoughts, but internalizing its counsel during the pain-filled, burden-laden, fear-producing moments of my life is what makes the lasting difference.

Whether you prance about in a top hat, dance playfully in a derby, or slink to the corner in a dunce's cap, life isn't about your headgear but your heart and your mind. Christ offers you all that you need and more; it's up to you to receive it and then to live as those who believe it.

I once thought I would die in my home, consumed by my fears. I never dreamed that one day I would have the privilege of broadcasting throughout the land God's love to others. We, dear ones, are limited in every way, but we must remember that God is limitless. When the Holy Spirit changed my mind—about God, myself, and others—through the truths of Scripture, I mentally stepped away from my screaming fears and entered into His calming peace.

If you're reading this book and have never received Christ as your personal Savior, I invite you to ask Him into your life. A simple prayer will work just fine. "Lord Jesus, come into my life, forgive my sins, and teach me to think and live Your way."

Not only will He immediately respond, but the Lord also will place on your head the helmet of salvation to help protect your mind from the enemy's lies and as a reminder of the decision you have made to trust Christ.

When a single soul bends her knee for the first time acknowledging Jesus, all of heaven celebrates. I wonder if angels have hats to throw? Maybe that's where the rest of us come in. C'mon, sisters in Christ, grab a hat, and give it a holy toss toward heaven to celebrate the Savior and His children.

As we retrieve our hats, may it be with a renewed commitment to think God's way. For in doing so, we find ourselves thinking outside our boxes and into a divine realm. This allows us to "put on" the mind of Christ, and as He becomes our Counselor, we then can make powerful decisions based on truth and love. And here's the crowning moment: When we think God's way, we not only become wiser but also emotionally steady. I don't know how you feel about that, but I'm ecstatic! Consider that together we can become—and are—influential women of faith, making amazing contributions to our families and to society. Uh-oh, I feel another hat-throwing moment coming on. Yahoo!